How to Dazzle at

Reading for Meaning

Irene Yates

Brilliant
PUBLICATIONS

We hope you and your class enjoy using this book. Other books in the series include:

English Titles

How to Dazzle at Grammar	978 1 897675 46 5
How to Dazzle at Writing	978 1 897675 45 8
How to Dazzle at Reading	978 1 897675 44 1
How to Dazzle at Spelling	978 1 897675 47 2
How to Dazzle at Macbeth	978 1 897675 93 9
How to Dazzle at Twelfth Night	978 1 903853 34 4
How to Dazzle at Romeo and Juliet	978 1 897675 92 2

Maths Titles

How to Dazzle at Oral and Mental Starters	978 1 903853 10 8
How to Dazzle at Algebra	978 1 903853 12 2
How to Dazzle at Written Calculations	978 1 903853 11 5
How to Dazzle at Maths Crosswords (Book 1)	978 1 903853 38 2
How to Dazzle at Maths Crosswords (Book 2)	978 1 903853 39 9

Science Titles

How to Dazzle at Being a Scientist	978 1 897675 52 6
How to Dazzle at Scientific Enquiry	978 1 903853 15 3

Other Titles

How to Dazzle at Beginning Mapskills	978 1 903853 58 0
How to Dazzle at Information Technology	978 1 897675 67 0

To find out more details on any of our resources, please log onto our website: www.brilliantpublications.co.uk.

Published by Brilliant Publications,
Unit 10, Sparrow Hall Farm,
Edlesborough, Dunstable, Bedfordshire LU6 2ES

email: info@brilliantpublications.co.uk
website: www.brilliantpublications.co.uk
Tel: 01525 222292

The name Brilliant Publications and its logo are registered trademarks.

Written by Irene Yates
Illustrated by Lynda Murray

© Irene Yates 1999
Printed ISBN 978 1 897675 51 9
ebook ISBN 978 0 85747 074 4

First published 1999. Reprinted 2001 and 2005, 2009.
Printed in the UK
10 9 8 7 6 5 4

Contents

Introduction

How to Dazzle at Reading for Meaning contains 40 photocopiable ideas for use with 9-14 year olds who are working at Levels 1 – 3 of the National Curriculum in English. The activities are presented in an age-appropriate manner and provide a flexible, but structured, resource for helping pupils to build up an understanding of what they are reading. The tasks break down into three definite strategies to provide activities to develop abilities in:

•   sequencing
•   cloze procedure
•   comprehension

Each of these three strategies has tasks at letter, word, sentence and paragraph level. It is hoped that all of the text in the main activities and the Add-ons will be seen as an extension for comprehension development, so that the teacher gives the pupil time to assimilate the instructions before embarking on the tasks.

Many of the words in the texts can be identified as 'high frequency' and 'medium frequency' words. This is to help pupils to become familiar with this vocabulary in order to reinforce it.

The emphasis with all of the sheets, at all times, should be 'Does what you read make sense?'. If is doesn't, then the pupil is making reading errors. They can use all kinds of cues and strategies to help them to decode the words, of course, but the key element is always 'meaning'. If they 'get stuck' they should be encouraged to 'have a go' and think for themselves what might make sense. They can then use decoding techniques to see if their 'guess' might be right. If it is, they should be praised. The fact that they have 'understood' and 'made meaning' out of the text should be a cause for celebration.

Often these pupils have built up a concept that learning to read is all about decoding, and do not realize that if they can get at the meaning first some of the words they find so elusive will fall into place. It sometimes comes as a complete surprise that they can actually be allowed to 'guess at' a word rather than break it down into bits and try to put it back together again. This skill of 'guessing' or predicting is one to be encouraged for it can make all the difference to a failing reader and boost his or her confidence enormously. It goes without saying that boosted confidence leads to boosted self-esteem, which leads to motivation, which leads to perseverance, which leads, eventually, to success.

Part of the disaffection of pupils with special needs is the misery of failing time after time. The sheets are designed, with information and questioning, to help those pupils to experience success and achievement. The expectation that the pupil *will* achieve will help to build confidence and competence.

The tasks in this book are kept fairly short, to facilitate concentration. The text on the pages is kept to a minimum, and the content of the pages is applied to contexts that the pupils will find motivating. In many cases there is an element of puzzle or competition to the activities to provide greater motivation. The Add-ons at the end of each task are to provide reinforcement and to enable the pupils to use the skill they have learned in a functional way.

How to use the book

The activity pages are designed to supplement any English language activities you pursue in the classroom. They are intended to add to your pupils' knowledge of how the English language works.

They can be used with individual pupils, pairs or very small groups, as the need arises. The text on the pages has been kept as short as possible, so that reluctant or poorer readers will not feel swamped by 'words on the page'. For the same reason we have used white space and boxes, to help the pupils to understand the sheets easily, and to give them a measure of independence in working through them.

It is not the author's intention that a teacher should expect all the pupils to complete all the sheets, rather that the sheets be used with a flexible approach, so that the book will provide a bank of resources that will meet needs as they arise.

Many of the sheets can be modified and extended in very simple ways. The Add-ons can provide a good vehicle for discussion of what has been learned and how it can be applied.

The companion book to this one is *How to Dazzle at Reading*, which concentrates on the skills necessary for decoding. Together the two books can provide a balance which will help your pupils to gain fluency and confidence.

Pages 46-48 provide answers where they are definitive. Where the answers may be various or may be written in different ways, please ensure that they are grammatically correct, with appropriate punctuation, since this requirement is shown as an instruction on each task.

Match the word

Draw lines to match up each word with its correct meaning. (You can use a dictionary to help you.)

birthday	material made by pressing wood pulp
window	not big
clothes	the opposite of over
father	a hole in the wall, with glass
paper	not outside
second	part of your body
high	the day you were born
under	the one after first
small	things you wear
inside	what you think
thought	male parent
head	the opposite of low

Add-on
Put the words into alphabetical order.

Match the words

Draw lines to match up each word with its correct meaning.
(You can use a dictionary to help you.)

watch	not having
below	of great consequence
different	all
number	look at
without	noise
together	not the same
important	not dark
every	under, or lower than
sound	definite
upon	word or symbol for how many
sure	on
light	one with another

Add-on
Put the words into alphabetical order.

Which meaning?

**Draw lines to match these words with their correct meanings.
(You can use a dictionary to help you.)**

laugh	greater in quantity
push	carried away
tree	coming before or after
brother	express amusement
more	one more
took	be alive
old	thrust away
next	do something for someone
another	a tall kind of plant
help	belongs to you
live	a son of your parents
your	not young, or new

Add-on
Put the words into alphabetical order.

Match-up

Draw lines to match these words to their correct meanings. (You can use a dictionary to help you.)

night	more than one
water	lots
two	on one occasion only
down	opposite of front
once	at what time?
many	not day
little	word by which you are known
back	more than one person
here	opposite of up
when	liquid that comes out of taps
people	not there
name	small

Add-on
Put the words into alphabetical order.

What does it mean?

Read each word carefully. Decide what it means. Write a proper sentence for each word, explaining its meaning.

Example: **astronaut** – An astronaut is someone who explores space.

hovercraft

bulldozer

parachute

century

lumberjack

bicycle

Add-on
Look up these words in a dictionary: potter, walrus, kayak, florist.

Getting the meaning

Read each word carefully. Decide what it means. Write a proper sentence for each word, explaining its meaning.

Example:	**practise** – When you practise something, you do it over and over again.

powerful

greedy

tickle

queue

pilot

comical

Add-on
Look up these words in a dictionary: observe, feeble, chemist, remember.

Think of an opposite

**Read each word carefully. Decide what it means.
Write a word which means the opposite.**

hard	first
smooth	late
tall	real
sensible	ordinary
end	distant
odd	shy
sick	cold

(Words which mean the opposite are called 'antonyms').

Helpline
You can use
a dictionary to
help you.

Add-on
Check your words with a friend. Have you both chosen the same words?
Write down any other words that could be used.

Opposites

**Read each word carefully. Decide what it means.
Write a word which means the opposite.**

poor	large
found	cruel
awake	empty
night	same
young	bring
tidy	shut
cheerful	high

(Words which mean the opposite are called 'antonyms').

Helpline
Use a
dictionary to
help you.

Add-on
Choose three words from your list. Write a sentence using these words.

Almost the same

Read each word carefully. Decide what it means.
Write another word which means almost the same.

little		child	
lots		man	
cry		snatch	
smile		tell	
noise		warrior	
sad		old	
run		ask	

(Words which mean 'almost the same' are called 'synonyms').

Helpline
Use a thesaurus to help you.

Add-on
Choose five of your words. Write a word which means
the opposite for each one.

Very similar

Read each word carefully. Decide what it means. Write another word which means almost the same.

lively	careless
nasty	bold
listen	angry
inform	squabble
dread	shriek
nag	rapid
dull	groan

(Words which mean 'almost the same' are called 'synonyms').

Helpline
Use a thesaurus to help you.

Add-on
Check your list of words with a friend. Have you chosen the same words?
Write down any other words that you could use.

Family anagrams

These words are all words for people in a family. The letters are in the wrong order. Write the words with the letters in their right order.

umm	ngdartomreh
add	ngdartafreh
thobrer	ciene
nuat	phneew
etrssi	nso
niousc	reduatgh
lenuc	

Helpline
Use a dictionary
to help you.

Add-on
Write a description of one member of your own family.

Animal anagrams

These words are all words for animals. The letters are in the wrong order. Write the words with the letters in their right order.

ribd	gkaanoro
gtrllaiao	smeuo
gleea	arbze
tna	peehs
phdloni	noli
xfo	repntha

Helpline
Use a dictionary
to help you.

Add-on
Write a description of one of these animals.

What does it all mean?

Sometimes we say things that do not mean exactly what we say.
For example:

I'll have to fly or I'll be late – really means
I'll have to hurry up or I'll be late!

Write a sentence below each of these to say what they really mean.

The teacher told Sue to <u>pick her feet up</u>.

Miss Smith said Josh always had his <u>head in the clouds</u>.

David <u>ran into</u> a problem.

Keep it <u>under your hat</u>.

Pete <u>flew off the handle</u> when he got his work wrong.

Emma wanted to <u>follow in her father's footsteps</u>.

Rashid wouldn't let anybody <u>cramp his style</u>.

Add-on
Choose one of the sentences and write a short story around it.

Tell me again!

Sometimes we say things that do not mean exactly what we say.
For example:

> We'll have to get down to the nitty gritty – really means
> We'll have to understand the bare facts.

Write a sentence below each of these to say what they really mean.

Gary was <u>dressed up to the nines</u>.

Sarah thought Jo was <u>as mad as a hatter</u>.

Anwar could see them <u>keeping an eye on him</u>.

Pete said the game <u>went like a dream</u>.

Jasbir didn't quite <u>get the drift</u> of the lesson.

Sonny had <u>money to burn</u>.

Danny was <u>spoiling for a fight</u>.

Add-on
Choose one of the sentences and write a short story around it.

Is this true?

Read the following sentences. Some are true. Some are not true. If the sentence is true, write YES by it. If the sentence is not true, write NO by it.

	YES or NO
1 Whales live in water.	
2 Cats eat carrots.	
3 Dogs can talk.	
4 Wet paint is sticky.	
5 Ireland is part of the British Isles.	
6 America is a city.	
7 Three quarters is more than one whole.	
8 Frogs are mammals.	
9 Aeroplanes run on tracks.	
10 A bus carries passengers.	

Add-on
Think up four statements of your own, two true and two untrue. Try them on a friend.

Yes or no?

Read the following sentences. Some are true. Some are not true. If the sentence is true, write YES by it. If the sentence is not true, write NO by it

Helpline
You can use a dictionary to help you.

	YES or NO
1 Clocks have faces.	
2 Kangaroos have tusks.	
3 Sydney is a country.	
4 There are thirteen players in a football team.	
5 Tap, line and ballet are all kinds of dance.	
6 An elephant is smaller than a hamster.	
7 Your mother's mother is your aunt.	
8 It always snows every day in January.	
9 Sunday comes between Saturday and Monday.	
10 A river is bigger than a stream.	

Add-on
Think up four statements of your own, two true and two untrue. Try them on a friend.

Crazy sentences

The words in these sentences are in the wrong order. Read them carefully. Write each sentence out again, correctly. Don't forget to put in full stops and capital letters!

1   an sports way are healthy keep to and fit excellent

2   of form transport cars a are

3   from anything we learn books can

4   before August comes September

5   many is of one Christmas festivals great

6   nine have cats supposed are to lives

7   four Games the are Olympic years every held

8   equal have sides squares four four equal and angles

Add-on
Write two mixed-up sentences of your own. Get a friend to put them right.

Get it in order

**The words in these sentences are in the wrong order.
Read them carefully. Write each sentence out again, correctly.
Don't forget to put in full stops and capital letters.**

1 world changed computers have the

2 reach top the team will our

3 in training keep you to have win to

4 animals are largest the land elephants

5 tell past fossils us the about

6 nearly blue extinct the whale is

7 travel atmosphere spaceships designed outside the are to earth's

8 is very a healthy swimming recreation

Add-on
Write two mixed-up
sentences of
your own.
Get a friend to put
them right.

Make it make sense

Read the paragraph carefully. Some of the words are in the wrong order. Decide what each sentence should say and write them with the words in the right order.

How March got its name

In Ancient Rome, March first the was month the of year. It was

named after Mars, of God the War. Mars was also the farming of

God. March is the month of the God Mars because the Ancient

Roman people farming and war loved.

Write the paragraph correctly here.

Add-on
Use a reference book to find out how January got its name.

Making sense

Read the paragraph carefully. Some of the words are in the wrong order. Decide what each sentence should say and write them with the words in the right order.

Hadrian's wall

Hundreds years of ago, the Romans built a wall across the

narrowest of part Britain, from the River Tyne the to Solway Firth.

The emperor Hadrian built it keep the to Scots tribes of out England.

Hadrian's was wall seventy-three miles long six took and years to

build.

Write the paragraph correctly here.

Add-on
Use a reference book to find out about the 'mile castles' built
on Hadrian's Wall.

Animal allsorts

Read the sentences carefully. Fill in the gaps. (You can use a dictionary to help you if you want to.)

1   An eagle is a large, wild, meat-eating __ __ __ __ .

2   A cheetah is a large, spotted member of the __ __ __ family.

3   A chipmunk is a North American ground __ __ __ __ __ __ __ __ .

4   St. Bernard, Poodle and Labrador are all common breeds of __ __ __ .

5   __ __ __ __ live only in water.

6   A baboon is a medium-sized __ __ __ __ __ __ .

7   A cockroach is an __ __ __ __ __ __ __ .

8   A muntjac is a small __ __ __ __ .

9   Crocodiles, lizards and snakes are all __ __ __ __ __ __ __ __ __ .

10 A porpoise is a small __ __ __ __ __ __ .

Add-on
Choose one animal to look up and read about in a reference book.

Lucky for some

Read the piece carefully. Fill in the gaps.

Lots of people __ __ __ __ __ that some things bring them good luck

and some things bring them __ __ __ luck.

It is __ __ __ __ __ __ __ __ to be lucky to find a four-leaf clover.

The superstition __ __ __ __ __ with the story that when Eve was

__ __ __ __ away from the Garden of Eden, she __ __ __ __ a

four-leaf clover with her as a bit of green from the garden. It became

known as a sign of __ __ __ __ luck.

Some people __ __ __ __ __ that horseshoes are lucky, and that

they have magic powers. Even the ancient Romans

__ __ __ __ __ __ __ it was good fortune to find a cast-off

horseshoe.

A broken mirror is supposed to bring bad __ __ __ __ for seven

years. It is also supposed to be __ __ __ __ __ __ __ to walk under a

ladder.

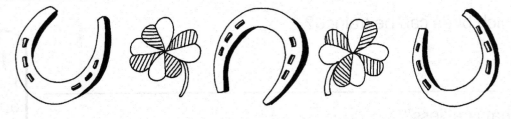

Add-on
Learn how to spell these words: superstition, fortune, luck, magic.

Birds of prey

Read the piece carefully. Fill in the gaps.

A falcon is a __ __ __ __ of prey. It catches other animals __ __ __

food. Falcons have long, pointed wings __ __ __ a notch like a tooth

in the cutting edge __ __ their beak.

A bird __ __ __ __ is strong enough and clever __ __ __ __ __ __

to hunt can easily __ __ trained. This kind of training __ __ called

'falconry'. The __ __ __ __ __ trained are usually falcons or hawks.

The trainer, who is called a 'falconer', wears a thick leather glove.

He __ __ __ a hood for the __ __ __ __ __ __ and fastens a short

leather strap, called a jess, round the legs __ __ the bird.

Answer the questions.

What does a falcon eat?

_____

What is falconry?

_____

Which birds can be trained?

_____

What is a 'jess'?

_____

> ## Add-on
> Find out more about falconry from the computer or your library.

The world's largest animal

Read the piece carefully. Fill in the gaps.

The blue whale __ __ the largest animal in the world. It is not a

__ __ __ __ , it is a mammal that lives in __ __ __ __ __ . A baby

__ __ __ __ __ is born alive and feeds on its mother's milk.

Whales have lungs __ __ __ __ humans, not gills like

__ __ __ __ . Their tails are __ __ __ __ __ __ flukes.

Blue whales have two blowholes at the top of their __ __ __ __

so that they can __ __ __ __ __ __ __ at the water's surface.

Answer the questions.

What is the world's largest animal?

_____

How is a baby whale born?

_____

Why do whales have blowholes?

_____

What is a 'fluke'?

_____

Add-on
Find out more about whales from the computer or your library.

Interest in insects

Read the piece carefully. Fill in the gaps.

There __ __ __ between two million and four million different kinds

of insect. There are far too __ __ __ __ for any scientist to be able to

describe __ __ __ __ __ insect that exists today!

It would be impossible to guess __ __ __ many insects are alive on the

planet each single day. We could not even begin to imagine the vast

__ __ __ __ __ __ .

In a square metre of rich, most soil, you __ __ __ __ __ find anything

from 500 to four or five thousand insects – if __ __ __ could see them!

Although we __ __ __ see butterflies, beetles, flies, etc. easily, most

insects are so tiny that we do not notice __ __ __ __ . Many can

__ __ __ __ be seen through a microscope. Most insects __ __ __ __

two things in common: their bodies are divided into three

__ __ __ __ __ , and they have six __ __ __ __ .

Add-on
Find out more about insects from the computer or your library.

Change the word

Read the following story. Look at the words and phrases that are underlined, then look at those in the Word Box.
Each of these words or phrases could be used instead of one that's underlined. Write the new words underneath the old words.

The Jones family were going <u>away</u>. Their suitcases were <u>packed</u> in

plenty of time. They had to <u>take</u> a bus into the city, then a coach to

the airport. At the airport there was a <u>girl</u> to meet them and <u>tell</u> them

where they had to go. She <u>told</u> them where to check-in.

They had to show their passports and <u>get</u> their suitcases weighed.

The check-in man made sure they had <u>good</u> seats and were going

to be able to <u>sit</u> together. The boys were <u>hungry</u>. Mum said, 'There

will be <u>something to eat</u> on the plane. You won't have to wait long.'

But they were still hungry, so she <u>gave</u> them some <u>money</u> to buy a

burger before their flight was called.

Word Box

cash	a meal	woman	on holiday	advise
catch	stay	have	starving	handed
showed	ready	comfortable		

Helpline
Watch out! The words in the Word Box are not in the right order!

Add-on
Write the story out again on another sheet of paper with its new words.
Check that it makes sense.

All change!

Read the following story. Look at the words and phrases that are underlined, then look at those in the Word Box.
Each of these words or phrases could be used instead of one that's underlined. Write the new words underneath the old words.

It was <u>supermarket</u> night. Danny wanted to stay <u>in</u> and watch the big film. Mum <u>said</u> he'd have to come, <u>too</u>. She needed his <u>help</u> to <u>pack</u> the shopping into the car.

Danny <u>sulked</u> for a bit but he soon <u>got over it</u>. First, he piled fruit into the trolley. Then he put in a mountain of pizzas and <u>loads</u> of ice-cream. Mum didn't seem to <u>mind</u>. She was just <u>pleased</u> he was helping. 'Thanks, Danny,' she said. 'I'm sorry you missed your <u>film</u>.'

Danny just <u>grinned</u> – he'd videoed it anyway!

Word Box				
told him	care	lots	laughed	programme
as well	glad	shopping	assistance	cheered up
load	home	pulled a face		

Helpline
Watch out! The words in the Word Box are not in the right order!

Add-on
Write the story out again on another sheet of paper with its new words.
Check that it makes sense.

How to Dazzle at Reading for Meaning
32

© Irene Yates
This page may be photocopied for use by the purchasing institution only.

Dinosaurs

Read the following passage. You will see that every seventh word is missing. Look at the words in the Word Box and work out which gap they fit into.

Dinosaurs lived on earth about 230 _____ years ago,

lasting about 165 million _____. Dinosaurs were huge reptiles.

The dinosaurs _____ mostly on land, although some of

_____ went into the water of rivers, _____ and swamps.

They never went into _____ sea.

Some dinosaurs were carnivores, that _____ they ate meat and

some were _____ , that means they were plant-

eaters. Some _____ on two feet and some on _____.

They were all cold-blooded, and most _____ scaly skins.

The brontosaurus was one _____ the largest dinosaurs. It had a

_____ head at the end of a _____ long neck. Its body was

huge _____ it had a long tail. It _____ weighed

about thirty or forty tons.

Word Box

probably	four	lived	of
means	very	the	walked
years	million	lakes	small
herbivores	them	and	had

Add-on
Read the passage carefully to see if it makes sense.

How to Dazzle at Reading for Meaning
33

Flying colours

Read the following passage. You will see that every seventh word is missing. Look at the words in the Word Box and work out which gap they fit into.

People have always wanted to fly.

_____ of years ago people tried to _____

with wings made of chicken feathers. _____ jumped off high

buildings with their _____ and ended up with broken bones!

_____ 1783 two French brothers found out _____ hot air rises.

They thought that _____ they filled a balloon with hot _____ it

would rise into the air. _____ it would fly.

They made their _____ out of cloth and paper. They

_____ a fire with straw and wood _____ filled the balloon

with hot air. _____ balloon rose about 200 metres and

_____ about 3 km.

The next time _____ tried, they took a cockerel, a _____ and

a sheep. They flew for _____ eight minutes and landed safely.

Word Box

balloon	Hundreds	wings	Then	The
made	travelled	and	about	
duck	they	that	experiment	
In	air	if	They	

Add-on
Read the passage
carefully to see if it
makes sense.

Saved!

These sentences make up a story, but they are in the wrong order.

The car passed.

He grabbed the child's hand and pulled him back.

Steve was walking down the street.

Steve shouted to the child.

There was a car coming.

He saw a little child trying to cross the road.

Steve took the boy safely across the road.

Write them out in the correct order here.

1 _____

2 _____

3 _____

4 _____

5 _____

6 _____

7 _____

Here are some answers. Write the questions.

_____

Steve

_____

He grabbed the child's hand and pulled him back.

Add-on
Write the story again as if YOU were Steve or the boy.

I want a dog!

These sentences make up a story, but they are in the wrong order.

Mel made friends with an old couple who couldn't get about much.

She knew they couldn't have a dog at home.

Mel thought it was nearly as good as having a dog of her own.

Her dad was allergic to dogs.

Mel wanted a dog more than anything.

She took their dog for a walk every morning and every afternoon.

Write them out in the correct order here.

1 _____

2 _____

3 _____

4 _____

5 _____

6 _____

Here are some answers. Write the questions.

_____

Her dad was allergic to dogs.

_____

She made friends with an old couple and took their dog for walks.

_____

It was nearly as good as having a dog of her own.

Add-on
Write the story again as though YOU were Mel or one of the old couple.

Frog in the garden

These sentences make up a story, but they are in the wrong order.

Kevin hardly dared to breathe.

The thing moved again.

He stopped and stood very still.

Kevin was kicking a ball in the garden when he saw something move.

The frog jumped behind a stone and disappeared.

It seemed to be frightened.

Kevin realized it was a frog.

Write them out in the correct order here.

1 _____

2 _____

3 _____

4 _____

5 _____

6 _____

7 _____

Here are some answers. Write the questions.

_____

Kicking the ball in the garden.

_____

A frog.

Add-on
Write the story as though YOU were Kevin.

Spaceship

These sentences make up a story, but they are in the wrong order.

> She saw the spaceship open and three strange creatures come out.
>
> She leapt back into bed and hid under the duvet.
>
> It was absolutely silent and an eerie light glowed from it.
>
> Of course, the next day, nobody believed her.
>
> The spaceship landed in the middle of the night.
>
> Jane watched from her bedroom window.

Write them out in the correct order here.

1 _____

2 _____

3 _____

4 _____

5 _____

6 _____

Here are some answers. Write the questions.

_____

A spaceship landed.

_____

Three strange creatures came out.

_____

She leapt back into bed and hid under the duvet.

Add-on
Write the story as though YOU were Jane.

The story of the Cyclops

Read each sentence carefully. They are in the wrong order. Decide which order they should be in.

Helpline
Cut and paste the sentences if you want to.

He kept the sailors prisoner in a cave and began to pick them off one by one.
They landed on the island of the Cyclops.
The Cyclops was a giant with one eye in the middle of his forehead.
Odysseus thought they were doomed. How on earth could they escape?
The Cyclops was a giant with one eye in the middle of his forehead.
Odysseus and his men were sailing home to Ancient Greece.

Write them out correctly here, so that the story makes the best sense. Write the sentences in a paragraph.

Add-on
Read the story of how Odysseus tricked the Cyclops in a book of Ancient Greek myths.

The story of Icarus

Read each sentence carefully. They are in the wrong order. Decide which order they should be in.

Helpline
Cut and paste the sentences if you want to.

Icarus dropped into the sea and was drowned.
He warned Icarus not to fly too near the sun.
Icarus and his father had to eacape from the island of Crete before King Minos had them killed. But how?
Daedalus, the father, made two sets of wings, so that they could fly.
But Icarus ignored him and kept flying higher and higher.
The sun melted the wax. The wings fell apart.
He fastened the feathers together with wax.

Write them out correctly here, so that the story makes the best sense. Write the sentences in a paragraph.

Add-on
Read the story of Icarus in a book of Ancient Greek myths.

The Olympic Games

Read the passage carefully.

The Olympic Games started in Ancient Greece. They were held every four years, just as they are now. In those days, if there was a war on, the war stopped so that the Games could be held.

The Games were always held at the same place – the City of Olympia, near Athens, in Greece. You can go to the original Olympia now to see, and run on, the tracks. You can walk through the tunnels that the ancient athletes walked through. Today, the games are held in different cities, all over the world.

Women didn't take part in the original games, and were not really allowed even to watch but, today, women compete and receive the same medals as men.

Although the marathon came from Greece, it was not part of the original Games, nor were the Winter Olympic events such as skiing, skating or ice hockey. The weather in Ancient Greece was much too hot for such games.

Answer the questions. Remember to write your answers in proper sentences.

Where did the Olympic Games begin?

_____

How often were they played?

_____

What happened if there was a war on?

_____

Why didn't the Ancient Greeks have speed-skating championships?

_____

Add-on
Find out about the Olympic Games on a
computer or in the library.

Bird table

Here is a table showing how long it takes different kinds of birds' eggs to hatch out.

Type of bird	Number of days
ostrich	40 days
swallow	15 days
woodpecker	25 days
chicken	21 days
swan	35 days
robin	12 days
goose	28 days

Write a paragraph to show this information in sentences instead of as a table.

Helpline
Say which birds' eggs take the longest to hatch and which birds' eggs take the least time.

Add-on
Use a computer or an encylopedia to find out about hatching times for these birds: blackbird, wren, flamingo.

Can you do this?

Read the following instructions and do what they tell you.

1 Write, in capital letters, the letters from K to P in the alphabet, beginning at P and going backwards.

2 Write, in small letters, the letters from S to Z in the alphabet, beginning at Z and going backwards.

3 Write the months that have only 30 days. Write them in the correct order.

4 Write the numbers for:
   a) one tenth

   b) one ten thousandth

   _____

   _____

   c) one hundredth

   d) one millionth

   _____

   _____

5 Draw a clock that shows the time at a quarter past ten.

6 Draw a triangle above a rectangle.

Add-on
Write three similar instructions. Ask a friend to follow them.

Follow the instructions

Carry out the following instructions without making a mistake.

1 Write, in capital letters, the letters from F to L of the alphabet.

2 Write, in small letters, the letters from P to V of the alphabet.

3 Write the months that come between June and September.

4 Write the numbers for:
   a) one thousand

   c) one hundred and ten thousand

   _____

   _____

   c) ten thousand

   d) half a million

   _____

   _____

5 Draw a clock that shows the time at twenty to seven.

6 Draw a square with a circle inside it.

Add-on
Write three similar instructions. Ask a friend to follow them.

Scrambled eggs on toast

Look at the pictures. Write the recipe.

Ingredients: (Food)

What you need: (Utensils)

What you do:

Add-on
Try out your recipe!

How to Dazzle at Reading for Meaning

Answer pages

The answers are given where there is a definitive or absolute answer. Where the pupils are asked to write their own sentences please check that they have given a correct answer and correct punctuation. They are reminded each time to write in proper sentences with capital letters and full stops.

Match the word.................................... page 6

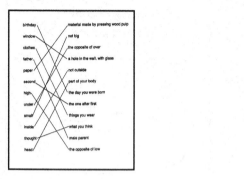

Match the words.................................. page 7

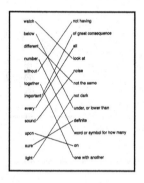

Which meaning?................................... page 8

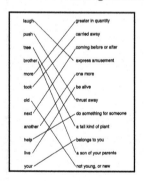

Match-up... page 9

Family anagrams .... page 16

umm	mum
add	dad
thobrer	brother
nuat	aunt
etrssi	sister
niousc	cousin
lenuc	uncle
ngdartomreh	grandmother
ngdartafreh	grandfather
ciene	niece
phneew	nephew
nso	son
reduatgh	daughter

Animal anagrams .... page 17

ribd	bird
gtrllaiao	alligator
gleea	eagle
tna	ant
phdloni	dolphin
xfo	fox
gkaanoro	kangaroo
smeuo	mouse
arbza	zebra
peehs	sheep
noli	lion
repntha	panther

Is this true?...................................... page 20

1	Yes	6	No
2	No	7	No
3	No	8	No
4	Yes	9	No
5	Yes	10	Yes

Yes or no?... page 21

1	Yes	6	No
2	No	7	No
3	No	8	No
4	No	9	Yes
5	Yes	10	Yes

Crazy sentences .... page 22

1 Sports are an excellent way to keep fit and healthy.
2 Cars are a form of transport.
3 We can learn anything from books.
4 August comes before September.
5 Christmas is one of many great festivals.
6 Cats are supposed to have nine lives.
7 The Olympic Games are held every four years.

Crazy sentences (continued) ....
8   Squares have four equal sides and four equal angles.

Get it in order ....
1   Computers have changed the world.
2   Our team will reach the top.
3   You have to keep in training to win.
4   Elephants are the largest land animals.
5   Fossils tell us about the past.
6   The blue whale is nearly extinct.
7   Spaceships are designed to travel outside the earth's atmosphere.
8   Swimming is a very healthy recreation.

Make it make sense ....
In Ancient Rome, March was the first month of the year. It was named after Mars, the God of War. Mars was also the God of farming. March is the month of the God Mars because the Ancient Roman people loved farming and war.

Making sense ....
Hundreds of years ago, the Romans built a wall across the narrowest part of Britain, from the River Tyne to the Solway Firth. The emperor Hadrian built it to keep the Scots tribes out of England. Hadrian's wall was seventy-three miles long and took six years to build.

Animal allsorts ....
1   bird   6   monkey
2   cat   7   insect
3   squirrel   8   deer
4   dog   9   reptiles
5   fish   10 whale

Lucky for some ....
think
bad
supposed
began
sent
took
good
think
thought
luck
unlucky

Birds of prey ....
bird
for
and
of
that
enough
be
is
birds
has
falcon
of

The world's largest animal ....
is
fish
water
whale
like
fish
called
head
breathe

Interest in insects ....
are
many
every
how
number
could
you
can
them
only
have
parts
legs

Change the word ....
on holiday
ready
catch
woman
advise
showed
have
comfortable
stay
starving
a meal
handed
cash

All change! ....
shopping
home
told him
as well
assistance
load
pulled a face
cheered up
lots
care
glad
programme
laughed

Dinosaurs .... page 33
million
years
lived
them
lakes
the
means
herbivores
walked
four
had
of
small
very
and
probably

Flying colours .... page 34
Hundreds
experiment
They
wings
In
that
if
air
Then
balloon
made
and
The
travelled
they
duck
about

Saved! .... page 35
1 Steve was walking down the street.
2 He saw a little child trying to cross the road.
3 There was a car coming.
4 Steve shouted to the child.
5 He grabbed the child's hand and pulled him back.
6 The car passed.
7 Steve took the boy safely across the road.

I want a dog! .... page 36
1 Mel wanted a dog more than anything.
2 Her dad was allergic to dogs.
3 She knew they couldn't have a dog at home.
4 Mel made friends with an old couple who couldn't get about much.
5 She took their dog for a walk every morning and every afternoon.
6 Mel thought it was nearly as good as having a dog of her own.

Frog in the garden .... page 37
1 Kevin was kicking a ball in the garden when he saw something move.
2 He stopped and stood very still.
3 The thing moved again.
4 Kevin realized it was a frog.
5 It seemed to be frightened.
6 Kevin hardly dared to breathe.
7 The frog jumped behind a stone and disappeared.

Spaceship .... page 38
1 The spaceship landed in the middle of the night.
2 It was absolutely silent and an eerie light glowed from it.
3 Jane watched from her bedroom window.
4 She saw the spaceship open and three strange creatures come out.
5 She leapt back into bed and hid under the duvet.
6 Of course, the next day, nobody believed her.

The story of Cyclops .... page 39
Odysseus and his men were sailing home to Ancient Greece. They landed on the island of the Cyclops. The Cyclops was a giant with one eye in the middle of his forehead. He kept the sailors prisoner in a cave and bagan to pick them off one by one. Odysseus thought they were doomed. How on earth could they escape?

The story of Icarus .... page 40
Icarus and his father had to escape from the island of Crete before King Minos had them killed. But how? Daedalus, the father, made two sets of wings so that they could fly. He fastened the feathers together with wax. He warned Icaurs not to fly too near the sun. But Icarus ignored him and kept flying higher and higher. The sun melted the wax. The wings fell apart. Icarus dropped into the sea and was drowned.

Can you do this? .... page 43
1 PONMLK
2 zyxwvuts
3 April, June, September, November
4 a) 1/10   b) 1/10,000   c) 1/100
  d) 1/1,000,000
5   6

Follow the instructions ....page 44
1 FGHIJKL
2 pqrstuv
3 July, August
4 a) 1,000   b) 110,000   c) 10,000
  d) 500,000
5   6